Gavin Bantock

Anhaga

six poems translated
from the Anglo-Saxon

Anvil Press Poetry
associated with
Routledge & Kegan Paul

First published in 1972
by Anvil Press Poetry
69 King George Street London SE 10
Distributed by Routledge & Kegan Paul Ltd
SBN 900977-34-5

Fifty numbered copies of this edition
have been signed by the author
SBN 900977-35-3

Printed in England by
Latimer Trend & Co Ltd, Whitstable

to M. O.

Wita sceal geþyldig

ACKNOWLEDGMENTS

Some of these translations have previously appeared in *New Measure, Peacock* and *Oxymoron*

PREFACE

The world of men is a dark place. The past has been a happier time. For the ruined city there is no future, the wife of Wulf is sick with grief and the ousted minstrel has only faint hopes. The Wanderer and the Seafarer have suffered bitterly, but Christ brings them consolation; and, finally, an unforgettable dream fills the mind of a lonely man with the lasting glory of God. In these six poems, we may see how the transience of much-loved worldly things gradually gives way to the permanence claimed by the Christian faith.

CONTENTS

THE RUIN

This wall of stones alone hath splendour;
the city buildings stand shattered, broken by fate:
the work of the giants crumbles away . . .

Roofs are fallen, towers ruined, and the barred gate
plundered. There is frost on the mortar.
The storm-shield, warped and torn apart, hangs
undermined with age.
        The earth's grip held back
the master-builders: they perished and passed away.
It was the earth's hard grasp,
while a hundred generations of men departed . . .

        Often this wall,
red-stained and grey with lichen, withstood
one kingdom after another, and remained
standing under the storms . . .

        Now the high curve is ruined:
it moulders still, an ancient work
marred with encrustments of mud . . .

        The heart moved,
urging a swift resolve, and thus resolved, men
bound the wall-foundation with wires intricate with ring
wonderfully together.

        Bright were the halls of the city,
many a bathing hall, high costly gables;
there was great sound of war preparation,
and many a mead-hall full of the joy of men

– till fate changed that.

Men cringed,
slaughtered far and wide;
days of decline came: death
snatched all battle-shrewd men:
wasted their war-strongholds;
the city crumbled away . . .
whole armies of men who came to rebuild it
fell dead to the earth . . .

Therefore these buildings
grow desolate . . . and the tiles
part from this red-curved roofwork of wood:
the ruin falls to the ground,
shattered to a mound of stones, where formerly
many a warrior, glad of heart and bright with gold,
adorned with splendour, proud and joyful with wine,
shone with war-trappings,
and gazed on treasures, on silver, on precious stones,
on wealth, possessions, ai! on precious stones;
on this bright city of the broad kingdom.

Bright buildings stood once . . .
the hot stream flowed wide and welming:
a wall enclosed all in its bright bosom . . .
there were the baths in the city's heart . . .
that was excellent . . .
the hot streams were then able to pour
over the grey stones . . . and under . . .
up to the round pond . . .
there were the hot baths . . .
then is . . .
that is a noble thing . . .
how the city . . .

WULF

To *my* people it would be as if they were given a gift.
But will *they* welcome him,
                                        if he comes among them?

        It is not so with us.

I wait upon one island,
                                        Wulf on another
bound fast all round with fens,
where there dwell men intent upon murder.
Will they welcome him,
                                        if he comes among them?

        It is not so with us.

Full of hope, with my Wulf,
I withstood far wanderings.
When it was rainy weather and I sat crying,
when the battle-shrewd man covered me with his arms,
it was such delight to me,
                                        but it was also pain . . .

Wulf, my Wulf, my thoughts of you
and your seldom coming sicken me:
my heart mourns, having no hunger . . .

Do you hear, Eadwacer?
Wulf shall carry off our child to the woods . . .

It is easy to tear apart what was never joined –
the song of us two together.

DEOR

Weland endured affliction because of the snake-rings:
he, strong-minded man,
had sorrow as companion, and longing, and suffered
winter-cold misery, finding woe often
after Nithad laid him in fetters –
lithe leather-bonds binding a better man.

That has passed. So may this.

The death of her brothers was not such
anguish in Beadohilde as her own predicament –
that clearly she was with child. . . she was too shocked
even to think clearly what might happen.

That has passed. So may this.

We have heard that the Geat's lamentations
for the lady Mathilde were groundless,
that his love-sorrow snatched all sleep from him.

That has passed. So may this.

It was known to many that Theodric
ruled for thirty years the city of the Maerings.

That has passed. So may this.

We have heard of the wolf-like thoughts of Eormanric
who far and wide ruled the people of the Goths' kingdom:
he was a grim king:
many a warrior sat gripped with sorrow,

expecting disaster. Long enough they wished
the kingdom overwhelmed.

That has passed. So may this.

A sorrow-burdened man sits, done out of joy:
he broods in heart,
and the multitude of his sorrows seems endless.
He may then think that the wise Lord Himself
has altered the world's history enough,
showing honour and certain fame to some,
and to some a multitude of woes.

Of myself I will say this:

Once I was minstrel of the Heodenings,
dear to my Lord.

Deor was my name.
Many years I had good employment and a kind lord
till Heorrenda, a man skilled in song,
received the position my lord formerly gave to me.

That has passed. So may this.

THE WANDERER

"Often the solitary man waits for God's mercy,
though he for a long while in sorrowful mood
has to stir back the rime-cold ocean
with oars, with the strength of his own hands . . .
to go in the tracks of exile over the sea. Fate –
that is relentless."

Thus remembering
the hardship of cruel slaughters
and the fall of kinsmen friends,
the wanderer spoke:

"Often in the early mornings
alone I have to bewail my grief:
now there is no one living to whom
I dare clearly open my mind.

"In truth I know
that in man it is excellent conduct
to bind fast the heart's lock,
to govern the mind's hoard-chamber,
to think, however, as he will.

"One who is
weary of heart may not withstand fate;
nor may the fierce heart glean help,
because, sorry and yet keen for glory, it is often
bound fast in its breast-chamber.

"Thus I,
so often weary with sorrow,

deprived of my native land
and far from free kinsmen,
have to bind my heart with fetters . . .
ever since my gold-friend and lord of former years
was laid in a dark chamber of earth . . .

"And sad with winter, I went away
over the frost-bound waves, and drearily
sought in halls for a giver of treasure – a lord –
sought where far or near I might find
anyone in a mead-hall who would love me,
who would cheer my friendlessness
and entice me with joys.

"He who knows
knows how cruel a companion sorrow is
to him who has no loving protectors with him:
the path of exile is his . . . No coiled gold,
no earthly riches, only the cold
of the heart's chamber . . . He remembers
the men of the halls and the receiving of treasure,
how his lord entertained him in his youth
at the feasts . . . All joy comes to an end.

"For he who knows
shall long go without dear lord's counsel.

"When sorrow and sleep
bind down a wretched exile,
it seems to him in mind
that he embraces and kisses his lord,
and lays his hands and head on that man's knee,
when in former days he sat on his throne . . .
long before . . .

"Then afterwards
the friendless man wakens and sees
the dark ways before him . . . sea-birds
batheing, and spreading their feathers . . .
rime-frost . . . and snow falling . . . mingled with hail.
There is a wound in the heavy heart,
grief over those he loves.

"Sorrow is renewed
when memory of kinsmen crosses his mind;
he greets them with joy, eagerly thinks of them . . .
But these companions of men swim away again
from his mind; the soul of those
who seem to float before him
does not bring there many of the familiar voices.

"Grief is renewed
in him who often sends his weary mind
yearning back over the frost-bound waves . . .
Therefore I cannot imagine anything in this world
which does not darken my mind
when I think of all the life of men –
how suddenly they pass from the hall-floors,
those high-spirited kinsmen!

"Thus each day
the world diminishes . . ."

Indeed, a man may not become wise
before he has had his number of years in the world.

A man has to be patient,
and must not be over-passionate,
nor too hasty of speech, nor too afraid,
or too glad; not too avaricious,

nor too eager to boast . . . if he is to become wise.

A man has to wait
– when he will speak proudly and boast –
until he knows which way
the thoughts of his mind will turn.

A wise man will understand
how unearthly it will seem
when all the wealth of this world stands devastated –
as even now stand various walls in this world,
blown upon by the winds,
covered with rime-frost . . . ruined dwellings . . .

Wine-halls crumble; kings lie deprived of happiness;
all the proud host fall by the wall:
war destroyed some of them, took them far away;
a raven carried one far-off over the high sea;
the hoary wolf gave over another to death;
a sad-faced man hid another in a chamber of earth: –
thus did the Creator of men destroy this world,
until, free from the noise of citizens,
the old works of the giants stood idle . . .

Then he who has wisely thought
and deeply considered the foundation of this dark life,
often turns his mind far back
onto the multitude of slaughters,
speaking these words:

"Where have gone the horses?
Where the men? Where are the treasure-givers?
Where are the banquet-dwellings?
Where the joys of the hall?

"O bright cup!
O chain-mailed warrior! O glory of kings!
how the times have passed,
how they grow dark under the shades of night
as though they had never existed!

"The beloved host
now stands behind a wondrously high wall
shining with serpent-forms.
The strength of spears, weapons
greedy for slaughter, have destroyed mankind –
a glorious fate!

"And storms
beat these rocky slopes; falling storm
binds the earth with terror of winter,
when darkness comes . . .
The shadow of night grows dark –
the fierce hail-storm from the north
sends malice on men.

"All in the kingdom of earth is full of hardship;
the decrees of fate overthrow
the world under the heavens.

"Here is life,
here is friend, here is kinsman,
here is man – all gone now after the brief lending . . .
all the foundations of this earth become desolate . . ."

Thus he spoke, wise in mind,
and sat apart from those at council.

"Good is he who keeps his integrity,
and he who never too quickly shows

grief from his heart, unless he first knows
how to effect the remedy with courage.

"Blessed are they who seek kindness from Him,
consolation from the Father in Heaven,
where safety stands for us all."

THE SEAFARER

Driven to talk of myself, a true story,
I have to tell of journeys, and how I
bore the brunt of hard days with bitter
sorrow of heart, and went with my ship
through regions that whiten the hair, and there
felt the terrible under-sway of the waves.

I had to keep keen night-watch at my ship's prow
when it was driven along close under the cliffs.
My feet were constricted with cold,
gripped by the frost's cold irons; whereas the sorrows sighed
hot round my heart; and hunger within
tore at my body's nerves which were worn down by the sea.

The happiest man on earth cannot know how I,
wretched and most sad in the paths of exile,
moved through winters on the ice-ribbed sea
deprived of friend and kinsman . . .
hung around with icicles when hail was
dashed down in the storms . . .

There I heard nothing but the roaring
ice-edged waves of the sea;
there for my entertainment all the while
I had the song of the wild swan;
for the laughter of men –
the gannet's cry and sound of the curlew;
for mead-drink – a gull singing.

There storms battered the cliffs;
there the tern with icy feathers

answered them; often there
the eagle, with wings dew-drenched,
yelled round . . . no protecting kinsman there
to comfort my lonely mind.

In truth, those who know the good things of city life
will hardly believe it: they will know so
little of the sorrow of these wanderings –
they are arrogant and wine-crazed; while sleep-starved
I had to go the way of the sea.

The night-shadows darkened;
it snowed from the north; frost was
locked to the earth; hail fell –
the coldest kind of grain spread on the ground.

Therefore, now that I myself
venture out upon the towering seas
daring the tumult of the salt waves,
thoughts trouble my mind – even though
the longings of my heart
urge my spirit each time to go, so that
far from here I might seek those alien . . .

For there is no man on earth –
proud of heart, generous in gift-giving,
active in youth, brave in his deeds,
and serving a friendly lord – who has not
sorrow forever on his sea-voyaging;
thinking how the Lord will treat him on his way.

Thought of harp is not with him,
nor thought of accepting rings;
no delight in woman, no pleasure in this world;
nor in truth anything but the rising and falling of waves.

Anyone who hungers to hasten sea-wards
always has this longing . . .

The groves come out in blossom, and make
beautiful the dwellings of men,
brightening the meadows;
the world hastes onward: all things
urge the mind and heart to make the journey,
goading those who may intend to go
far out on the ways of the ocean.

Likewise the cuckoo warns with its sad voice:
the guardian of summer sings, foreboding
bitter sorrow in the heart's feelings.
The ordinary man, blessed with comfort,
cannot know what is suffered by those
men who move in the farthest tracks of exile.

Therefore now from my breast, my heart reaches out;
my spirit journeys with the sea, over the haunts of whales,
journeys far out into all the world's regions.
Full of longing it comes
back to me often . . .

That spirit, flying there alone,
yells and incites me onto the whale-road,
irresistibly over the expanses of the sea,
because the joys of God are more inspiring to me
than this dead life upon land,
so soon gone after the brief lending.

Earthly wealth is by no means eternal.
Always before a man's last hour,
three things are uncertain –
sickness, old-age or sword-hate: one of these

snatches life from the doomed man.

Therefore the best of fames is the praise
given to each man after his death,
which, before he goes on his way, he must earn
by good work on land against the malice of fiends,
and by good deeds against the Devil.
Then the children of men will praise him afterwards,
and his glory shall live with the angels,
and he shall abide in glory always,
sharing joy with the host.

Days have gone by, fraying
all the wealth of the world's kingdoms:
now there are no kings or emperors,
no gold-givers as in former times
when they did their greatest deeds of glory
and lived in their greatest fame.
All this splendour is ruined, and the joys of living
gone: weaker men dwell here, swaying a world
where joy is nothing more than pain.
Glory declines; and all splendour, like each man
now here on earth, ages and withers:
old age strikes him down, his face whitens,
grey-haired he mourns, knowing that his former friends,
sons of noble men, are laid in the ground.
Then when life leaves him, his body is not able
to swallow sweet things or feel sorrows:
nor can he raise up his hand, nor think with his mind.
Though his grave will shine with gold trappings,
and though his brother will bury with him
much treasure alongside his kinsmen,
none of these precious things can go with him.

Hoarding of gold in his lifetime will not help

a sinful man when his soul is hauled before
the presence of God's terrible power.

The power of the Lord is great,
for by Him the face of the earth changes;
He created the firm foundations,
the expanses of earth and the Kingdom above.

He who has no fear of the Lord is foolish:
death comes, sudden.
He who lives humbly is blessed:
mercy comes from the heavens!

The Lord created for man his mind:
therefore he should believe in God's power.
A man should govern his headstrong will,
and, trustworthy in his promises
and pure in his way of living, hold it firm.

Each man should act in moderation
towards both his enemy and his friend,
or he shall have misery . . . and though God will not,
full of fire or in conflagration burn up
the friend He has made,
Fate is stronger: and God is stronger
than the thought of any man.
Let us consider then where we shall have our last home,
and then reflect how we may arrive there;
and we may then strive to gain
entrance to that eternal happiness
where life finds its being in God's love
and in the joy of Heaven.

And therefore may the Holy Lord God of Glory
receive now our thanks:

for He has exalted us forever.

Amen.

THE DREAM OF THE CROSS

Ai! this is the dream I dreamt at midnight
when sleep had silenced the voices of men!

I saw a magnificent cross
borne aloft and tied up with light –
an intensely bright beam of wood
richly adorned with wonderful gold and jewels
shining out across the earth's width;
and five of the jewels stood fixed above the cross-beam!

Angels gathered: the constant
moving of time had shaped them into perfection;
they gazed upon the jewels:
this was indeed no gallow for criminals:
this was a sight for the eyes of earthly men;
and holy spirits and all the shining universe beheld it!

This cross, this tree of victory . . . I was stunned by it!
I, guilty of crimes and wounded by them,
saw this emblem adorned with streaming lights
shining most beautifully and decorated with gold.

I was afraid of this weird cross:
it seemed to fluctuate with streams of light
and with colours of all kinds:
now it was misted over with moisture,
drenched with flowing sweat and blood;
now it gleamed with precious things,
constantly changing . . .

But through that gold, in spite of its splendour,

I could perceive the former agony of Christ,
so that, on its right side, the cross
seemed to sweat with blood.
And I, lying there a long while,
looked at the cross of the Saviour's sorrow,
and then I heard it make sounds:
ai! that most precious cross of wood began to speak!

Many years ago . . . I still remember . . .
I was hewn down somewhere in the heart of a forest,
trunk severed from the roots,
seized by hostile foreign men,
made a spectacle of for their entertainment –
commanded to bear their criminals aloft.
Some of these men carried me on their shoulders
and set me down on a hill; and some of them
fastened me there into the ground.

Then I saw the Lord of Mankind
hastening eagerly towards me, to ascend me:
I dared not act against the word of the Lord –
I did not dare to bow down or collapse
though I saw the earth's whole width shudder.
I could have killed all those hostile men;
but I stood fast.

The young Saviour drew off his garments –
He that was Almighty God – and with strength of heart
firmly resolved, He rose up high upon the gallow-cross:
for He was eager to redeem Mankind.

I shook when the Hero embraced me;
yet I did not dare bow down to the earth
or fall down; no, I had to stand fast:
I had been set up as a cross; I was there

to raise up a great King – the Lord of Heaven!
I did not bow myself down.

They drove dark nails through me –
there were visible wounds upon me,
open wounds of malice;
but I dared not lash out at any of those
hostile men who mocked the two of us together.
I was all moistened with blood from that Man's side
when He gave up the spirit and passed from this world.

I had to bear with much hostile wrath on that hill:
I saw the God of Hosts cruelly outstretched there:
the radiant body of the Saviour was
covered by clouds with darkness;
and a shadow went forth, dark under the clouds.

All things created wept, mourning the fall of a King:
Christ was upon the cross.
Many came from afar, hurrying to the Lord.

I saw all this.
I was troubled with bitter sorrow;
yet very humbly and eagerly I bowed down
to be in reach of men's hands.
They took hold of that Almighty God
and moved Him from His bitter torment;
those brave men left me standing, glistening with moisture:
I was deeply wounded with spears.

They laid Him limb-weary down and stood at His head;
there they gazed on the Lord of Heaven;
and He rested Himself there awhile,
exhausted after the great agony.
They made Him a tomb, in the sight of His enemies –

they carved it from bright stone
and laid within it the Lord of Victories.

Then, in the evening, they sang Him a dirge,
and went away forlornly from the Illustrious Lord,
He, in the meantime, resting there without companion.

Yet we, weeping there for a long while,
stood still after hearing those good men's voices.

That Body, beautiful
dwelling place of life, cooled.

Then we were cut down to the earth –
that was a grim business:
we were buried in a deep pit;
but disciples of the Lord, friends,
heard I was there and clothed me with silver and gold.

Now you can understand, much-loved man,
that I have endured the actions of wicked men –
extreme sorrow; and now the time has come
when men and all this sublime creation
shall worship me far and wide, and shall
pray to Him in the name of this emblem.
Upon me the Son of God suffered for a time:
therefore now I tower gloriously under the sky,
and I can heal all men that fear Him through me.
Long ago I was made the hardest of torments,
loathed by the people, until I gave them,
gave to all who have voices, all men,
the way to the true way to life.
Ai! the Prince of Glory, the Guardian of Heaven's Kingdom,
even as He set Mary His Mother above all women and men,
honoured me above all the trees of the forest.

Now I command you, god-blessed man:
speak of your dream to all men; with your words
uncover the truth that this is the glorious tree-cross
on which God Almighty suffered for the long-past
deeds of Adam and the many sins of Mankind.

Then with a happy heart, I alone there
said to that cross my fervent prayers;
my soul longed to go forth; I felt most keen longing;
but there's joy in knowing that I now alone can seek
that cross of victory more often than all men,
and can honour it well. My will is strong to do that,
and with that cross rests my safety.
I never had many powerful friends on earth,
and they have gone away from the joys of this world;
they have looked for the King of Glory;
now they live in Heaven with the High Father,
and dwell in that glory. And each day,
I long for that time when the Lord's cross,
which I saw here on earth in my dream,
will fetch me back from this life
loaned to me for my brief span of years,
and take me then where there is much
joy in Heaven, where the Lord's people are
gathered together feasting in unending happiness;
and set me then where I also may thereafter
dwell in that glory and share the joy of the saints.

May the Lord, Who suffered here on earth on that cross
for the sins of men, be my friend:
for He has saved us, and He has given us life,
and He has given us a Heavenly home.